Looking at CANADA

Children skating in the heart of Quebec City

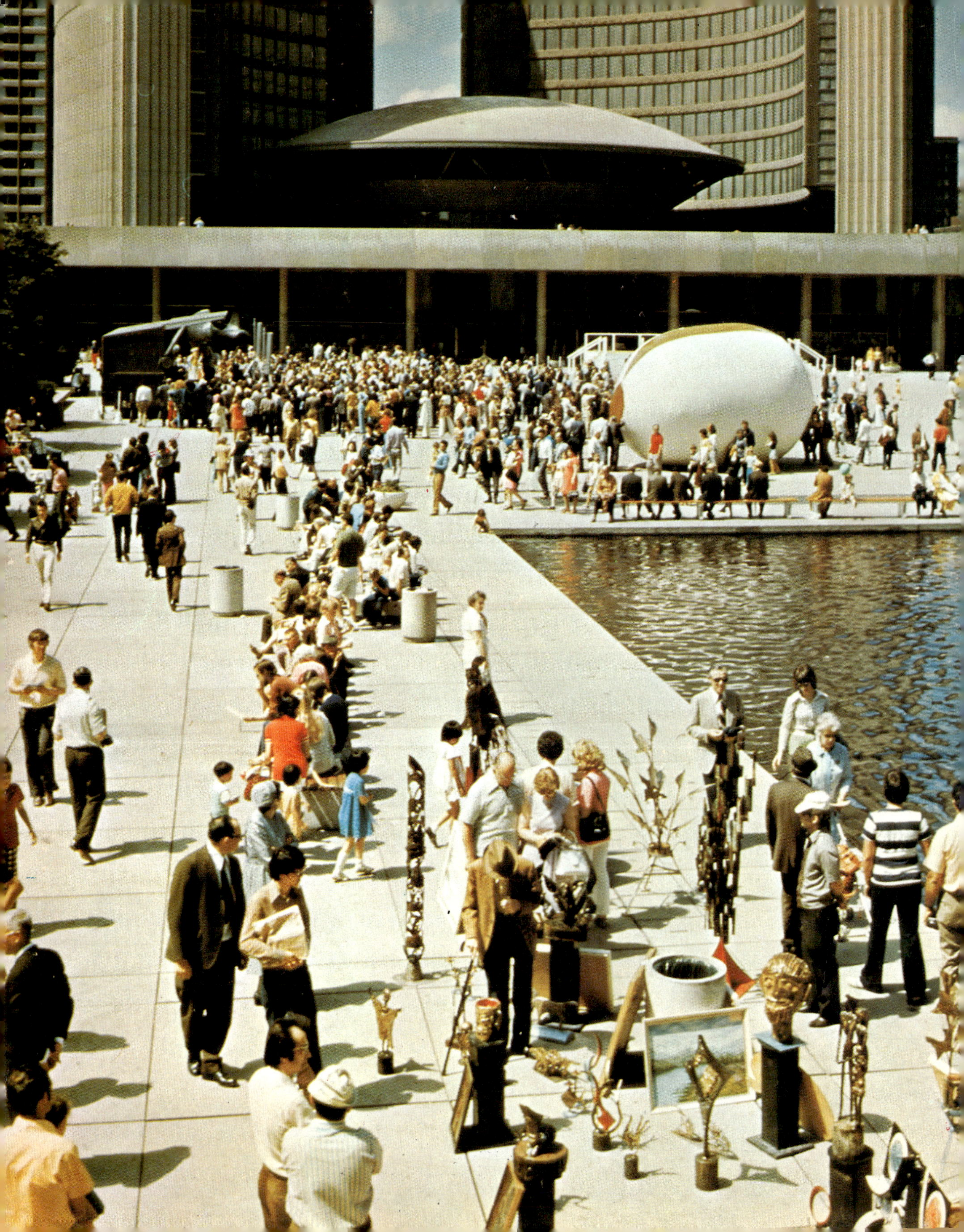

Looking at
CANADA

JOSEPHINE EARN

Adam and Charles Black   London

J. B. Lippincott Company   Philadelphia and New York

Art exhibition in Nathan Phillips Square, Toronto

Looking at Other Countries

Looking at HOLLAND
Looking at ITALY
Looking at GREECE
Looking at NORWAY
Looking at DENMARK
Looking at JAPAN
Looking at SPAIN
Looking at FRANCE

Looking at ISRAEL
Looking at SWEDEN
Looking at GERMANY
Looking at GREAT BRITAIN
Looking at BRAZIL
Looking at CHINA
Looking at NIGERIA
Looking at CANADA

Further titles in preparation

Grateful acknowledgement is made to the following for their permission to reproduce photographs:
Aerofilms 16c, 32
Vincent Brown cover b, 2, 8a, 16b, 17, 18, 28c, 33c, 37, 42, 43, 50, 51a, 59
Canadian Government Travel Bureau 6, 7, 10a and b, 13b, 14, 15, 19, 20a and b, 22, 23a, 25a, 29, 38, 39, 40a, 55, 56b and c, 60, 61b
Canadian Information Services cover a, 1, 5, 9b, 12a and b, 21a, 24a, b and c, 25b, 28a and b, 41a, 44b, 45a, 48a and b
J. Allan Cash 8a, 12c, 26, 27, 30a and b, 33a and b, 36a, 41b, 45b, 52c, 57a
Department of Trade and Commerce 52b
Robert Harding Associates 11, 35, 58
Hudson's Bay Company 13a
Jean Lauvaux 54a and b
Massey-Ferguson Limited 36c
National Film Board of Canada 16a, 37c, 44a and c, 45c, 49a and b, 52a
Newfoundland Department of Tourism 21b
J. Overell 34, 46a, 47, 51b
Public Service, Canada 53
Barbara Wace 9a and c, 23b, 31, 36b, 37b, 40b, 46b, 56a, 57b and c, 61a

The cover pictures show (a) musical ride by the Royal Canadian Mounted Police and (b) mountain scenery near Banff, Alberta

The maps on pages 62 and 63 were prepared by the Kater Print Company

U.S. Library of Congress Cataloging in Publication Data

Earn, Josephine.
   Looking at Canada.

   (Looking at other countries)
   Includes index.
   SUMMARY: Introduces the geography, people, history, cities, culture, and resources of Canada.
   1. Canada—Juvenile literature. [1. Canada] I. Title.
F1008.2.E27   971   76-8481
ISBN-0-397-31704-2

All rights reserved. No part of this publication may be reproduced, stored in any retrieval system, or transmitted, in any form or by any means, electronic, mechanical, photocopying, recording or otherwise, without the prior permission of A. & C. Black Ltd

ISBN 0 7136 1544 3 (British edition)

© 1976 A. & C. BLACK LTD, 35 BEDFORD ROW, LONDON WCIR 4JH
PRINTED IN GREAT BRITAIN BY
JARROLD & SONS LTD, NORWICH

CONTENTS

From Sea to Sea 6
The First Canadians 8
History 12
Ottawa and Government 17
Newfoundland 20
The Maritimes 22
Quebec 25
Ontario 31
The Prairie Provinces 35
The Territories 39
British Columbia 41
Daily Life in the Seasons 44
Sport 49
Homes 51
Education 53
Transport 56
Industry 58
The Canadian Wilderness 60
Map 62–63
Index 64

A chess set presented to Queen Elizabeth by Canadian Eskimos. The chessmen are carved from soapstone and the board is covered in sealskin

A gentle farming landscape in Prince Edward Island

From Sea to Sea

Canada is a rich and beautiful land, second only to the Soviet Union in size. It is slightly larger than the United States but forty times the size of Britain and eighteen times that of France. Bordered to the east and west by the Atlantic and Pacific oceans, it stretches from the boundary with the United States northward to the Arctic.

Because it is so far north, nearly all of Canada has a long cold winter and a short summer. Most of the people live in the south near the United States border, while two-thirds of the country remains sparsely populated because it is rocky, mountainous or extremely cold.

To the east are the rolling highlands, fertile valleys and rugged shoreline of the Atlantic coastal region. Inland lies the St Lawrence–Great Lakes lowland, a small fertile plain which attracted early settlers. Today it is the most heavily populated, intensively farmed and industrialized area of Canada.

Most of northern and central Canada, about half the country, is covered by a rocky wilderness known as the "Canadian Shield". The Shield is rich in forests, minerals and wildlife, and its thousands of lakes are teeming with fish.

West of the Canadian Shield stretch the Great Plains. The southern part, the Prairie, is famous for wheat growing. Between the Plains and the coast lie several mountain ranges of which the best known are the Rocky Mountains. The narrow Pacific coastal region is the only part of Canada with a temperate climate of mild winters and warm summers.

Canada's people have come from every country in the world. The early settlers had to combat hardships of climate and soil and intense loneliness in an empty land. Today's Canadians have the help of modern technology and communications, and seven out of ten of them live in cities and towns. Yet northern Canada is still a frontier region where pioneers face the challenge of the wilderness.

In September and October the leaves glow in crimson and gold

The First Canadians

The American Indians were the first people to live in Canada. Their ancestors came from Siberia more than twenty thousand years ago, crossing the strip of land which once joined Siberia to North America. When Columbus reached the Americas in 1492, he believed at first that he had found a new route to India and so he called the people living there "Indians".

The Indians depended for food on hunting, fishing and gathering wild plants and berries. In places where the summer was long enough, they grew crops such as corn (maize), beans and pumpkin. To help them survive the winter, they made a very nutritious food called "pemmican" from strips of dried meat, pounded to powder and mixed with hot fat and berries.

The Indians made their homes of logs, birchbark or animal skins and their clothing of skins or furs. People today use canoes, wooden toboggans and snowshoes and wear moccasins not very different from those made by the early Indians. The Pacific Coast Indians carved elaborate totem poles which stood in

A totem pole carved by Pacific Coast Indians

The American bison or "buffalo" provided the Prairie Indians with meat and skins

front of their homes. Countless towns, lakes and rivers in Canada have names of Indian origin and the name "Canada" itself is believed to come from an Indian word meaning "group of huts".

During the seventeenth and eighteenth centuries the arrival of Europeans in Canada began to change the Indian way of life. Explorers and fur traders depended on Indian guides. The Indians began to hunt fur-bearing animals to trade for weapons, tools and food, instead of making everything for themselves.

As towns and farms were established, farmers replaced the fur traders. The Indians were no longer free to travel across the land, hunting, fishing and camping wherever they liked.

On the Prairie, descendants of French fur traders who had married Indian women, were known as *Métis*. They were skilled buffalo hunters and they supplied the early colonists with meat and pemmican. When they saw that the large number of new settlers threatened their way of life, the Indians and Métis rose in rebellion in 1870 and again in 1885. The rebellions were defeated and Louis Riel, the Métis leader, was convicted of treason and hanged.

Drying strips of meat for pemmican

An Indian artist in Saskatchewan using old Indian designs for modern rugs

An Indian with the snowshoes he makes

Ceremonial costumes on display   Drum dancers at the Arctic Winter Games at Yellowknife

By the end of the nineteenth century land had been set aside in every part of Canada so that each band could live on its own reserve. Today there are about three hundred thousand Indians in Canada, most of them living on reserves under the protection of the Canadian Government. Some communities support themselves by farming, trapping, hunting and fishing. Indians who move to the cities often find it hard to adapt to modern life.

About seventeen thousand Eskimos or Innuit live in the Canadian Arctic. Their ancestors probably came from Siberia too, but later than the Indians. They were expert in living under Arctic conditions, their survival depending on their skill in hunting and fishing. Seal, walrus and caribou (the North American reindeer) supplied them with meat as well as with bone and ivory from which they made tools and weapons. No one has yet devised winter clothing warmer than the Eskimo *parka* and leggings, made of caribou skins.

The Eskimos fished from small boats or through holes in the ice. In summer they lived in tents of animal skins, and in winter they built a snow house.

In the nineteenth century missionaries, whaling ships and fur traders brought European ways to the Arctic. A few Canadian Eskimos still live in the old way, but more and more of them now live in modern prefabricated houses in permanent communities where the children can go to school. Adults make a living from trapping and fur trading or work in the small towns and weather stations which are now found in the Arctic. The snowmobile is replacing the sled and dog team as a means of transport.

Eskimos are superb craftsmen, carving exquisitely in wood, bone and ivory. Soapstone carvings of great beauty have been created by Eskimo artists for hundreds of years. Modern soapstone carvings are produced for sale and examples of them are found in many Canadian homes.

Today Eskimos like to be called "Innuit", meaning "men" in their language. Other familiar Eskimo words are *kayak*, *parka* and *igloo*.

Eskimo women with their children

A replica of the Habitation built by Champlain in 1605

This building at Sillery, Quebec, is probably the oldest in Canada, dating from 1657

History

Vikings from Iceland and Greenland sailed down the east coast of Canada in the eleventh century AD, but they did not settle permanently. In the fifteenth century European explorers came in search of a new route to India and China. John Cabot, sailing from England in 1497, discovered an offshore island (either Newfoundland or Cape Breton) and the rich fishing grounds of the Grand Banks. Jacques Cartier, the great French explorer, sailed up the St Lawrence River in 1535.

Throughout the sixteenth century Europeans fished off the east coast and the French began to trade with the Indians for furs. The profits from the fur trade prompted the French to establish colonies. Samuel de Champlain founded Acadia on the coast in 1604 and New France at Quebec on the St Lawrence River in 1608. The city of Montreal was founded in 1642. From New France explorers,

Scandinavian settlers built their log cabins of split tree trunks

The charter, granted by Charles II, which created the Hudson's Bay Company in 1670

fur traders and missionaries pressed inland as far as the western plains.

In the meantime the British landed in Hudson Bay and in 1670 they claimed a vast area of northwestern Canada for the British Crown. The Hudson's Bay Company set up a fur-trading system which soon began to rival that of the French.

In a series of wars the British and French fought for control of Canada. In 1759 the British won a decisive victory near Quebec City and in 1763 the Treaty of Paris confirmed British rule in Canada. Acadia became the colonies of Nova Scotia, New Brunswick and Prince Edward Island, while New France became known as Quebec.

A large group of English-speaking settlers, the United Empire Loyalists, came to Canada from the United States after the American Revolutionary War, because they wished to remain British. Many settled in the Upper St Lawrence Valley in what is now Ontario.

In the west exploration and fur trading extended to the Arctic and Pacific coasts. The small Red River Colony was founded on the Prairie in 1812, and British Columbia in the far west in 1858.

A sentry in 1866 uniform recreates colonial Canada for tourists at a fort in Fredericton, NB

In the War of 1812 Canadians turned back attacks from the United States. People became convinced that the colonies would be more secure and prosperous if they united. In 1864 the leaders of the colonies met at Charlottetown in Prince Edward Island and in Quebec City to discuss union. On 1 July 1867, Quebec, Ontario, Nova Scotia and New Brunswick united to become provinces of the Dominion of Canada within the British Empire.

After 1870 settlers began to move overland into western Canada. The Northwest Mounted Police Force (now the Royal Canadian Mounted Police) was founded in 1873 to enforce the law in the west. The fairness and discipline of the Mounties earned the respect of Indians and settlers alike. They prevented lawlessness and bloodshed of the kind that troubled the early days in the American West.

Manitoba became a province in 1870, British Columbia in 1871, Prince Edward Island in 1873, Alberta and Saskatchewan in 1905 and Newfoundland in 1949.

Mounties preparing a horse for a musical ride by brushing the national symbol, a maple leaf, on its rump

Candlemaking at the Black Creek Pioneer Village near Toronto. Canada has many museums like this where pioneer days are brought vividly to life

In 1867 the Government of Canada faced a tremendous task in trying to unify the huge country. A vast area of rock, lakes and muskeg (a kind of marsh made up of thick layers of decaying vegetation) separated the established settlements of eastern Canada from the Prairie. High mountains formed another great natural barrier between the Prairie and the Pacific Coast. The Canadian Pacific Railway, completed in 1885, crossed Canada from coast to coast and was a major factor in uniting the scattered areas of settlement. Thousands of immigrants were able to journey by rail to start a new life in the west.

After Confederation Canada moved steadily to full independence. Ties with Britain remain strong, and Canada is a partner in the British Commonwealth of Nations. She fought in both world wars on the side of Britain, the United States and their allies, and as a member of the United Nations Canada plays an active role in world affairs.

Crossing the border at Niagara Falls

New development in Edmonton, Alberta, one of Canada's rapidly growing cities

In the twentieth century Canada has developed rapidly as an industrial nation, except during the economic depression of the 1930s. Older Canadians have bitter memories of this time when thousands were unemployed and many people knew poverty and hunger. On the Prairie severe drought and plagues of grasshoppers caused crop failure and dreadful hardship for the farmers.

Since the Second World War Canada has prospered and immigrants have come from Britain, other European countries, and recently from Asia and the West Indies. Today twenty-two million people live in Canada and they enjoy the second highest standard of living in the world.

Canada and the United States have lived side by side in peace and friendship for over a hundred years, and the United States is Canada's most important trading partner. Every year thousands of tourists cross the long undefended border between the two countries.

Locks on the St Lawrence Seaway which was built jointly by Canada and the United States

Ottawa and Government

Ottawa is the capital city of Canada. It is beautifully situated on the Ottawa River which forms the boundary between Quebec and Ontario. Great care has been taken to plan the city's public buildings and spacious parks to make a proud and distinguished capital. The Rideau Canal which links the Ottawa River to Lake Ontario is now a pleasure waterway, with picturesque drives along its banks, and within the city the Canal is flanked by gardens. The Gatineau Hills, north of the city, provide a beautiful setting for sports and leisure both in summer and winter.

Queen Elizabeth II of Great Britain and Northern Ireland is also Queen of Canada. She is represented in Canada by the Governor General, a highly respected Canadian who performs all the ceremonial duties of head of state, and whose official residence, Rideau Hall, is in Ottawa.

The Rideau Canal, Ottawa

Canada has a parliamentary form of government on British lines, with two Houses of Parliament, the Senate and the House of Commons. Senators are appointed by the Governor General on the recommendation of the Prime Minister, and they serve until they retire at the age of seventy-five. The House of Commons is elected by Canadians who have reached the age of eighteen, and a general election has to be held at least every five

Changing the Guard on Parliament Hill. The Canadian flag is flying from the Peace Tower

The Canadian Tulip Festival

years. The leader of the political party with most seats in the House of Commons becomes Prime Minister. He governs the country with the help of his ministers who form the Cabinet.

Like the United States, Canada is a federation. The Government in Ottawa represents all Canadians and deals with matters concerning the whole country. Each province also has its own elected government whose leader is called a "premier". The Queen is represented in each province by a lieutenant-governor.

Many of the people working in Ottawa are employed by the Canadian Government or the embassies and legations of other countries. Ottawa attracts more tourists than any other part of the country. People come to see the Parliament buildings and the National Art Gallery, and they like to watch the Changing of the Guard on Parliament Hill. In May they come for the Canadian Tulip Festival. Every year Queen Juliana of the Netherlands sends sixteen thousand bulbs to the city in gratitude for the hospitality which she and her family received during the Second World War.

An "outport" clinging to the rocky coast of Newfoundland

Newfoundland

The most easterly province of Canada is Newfoundland, made up of the island of Newfoundland and mainland East Labrador. The Labrador current, flowing from the Arctic, makes the climate cold and foggy and brings huge icebergs which melt slowly in the coastal waters.

The first English-speaking settlers in North America came to the island of Newfoundland, attracted by the rich fishing grounds near by. The port city of St John's was founded in 1528. Fishermen from isolated villages on the rocky coast braved cold, fog and fierce storms to grasp a perilous living from the sea. There were few roads on the island and the fishing settlements or "outports" were reached only by sea.

Newfoundlanders have a proud and independent spirit. Most of them are descendants of settlers from the West of England, Scotland and Ireland. Their speech is

Fishing for giant tuna is a tourist attraction

distinctive, with words and sounds found nowhere else in Canada, and they have a rich store of traditional songs and stories.

Fishing is still a major industry and most of the people live near the coast. However, many have moved from the outports to larger towns where there are better schools and services, and as a result the traditional life of the outports is declining.

In most of the province the soil is poor and farms are small, often producing only enough food for the farmer and his family. In recent years lumbering, mining, hydro-electric development and manufacturing industries have increased. Even so, many Newfoundlanders move to other parts of Canada to find work.

Thousands of tourists come every summer to enjoy the charm and beauty of the island. Some places have unusually vivid names: for instance, Come by Chance, Heart's Content, Blow Me Down and Little Heart's Ease.

When the tide comes in, fish are caught in the meshes of this fish weir

The underground powerhouse of the Churchill Falls hydro-electric plant, the largest of its type in the world

The Maritimes

The Maritime Provinces of Nova Scotia, New Brunswick and Prince Edward Island face the Atlantic Ocean. The weather is often stormy and the winter snowfall heavy. The sea prevents extremes of temperature on the coast and Maritime ports do not freeze in winter. Fishing is an important industry, and tourists are attracted to the Maritimes by fine sandy beaches, splendid scenery and the region's long history.

The Maritimes have a small population, and industrial development has been slower than in some parts of Canada. Many Maritimers move to Ontario and Quebec to look for work, but those who remain value the quiet leisurely pace of their lives. French-speaking and English-speaking Canadians, many descended from the Acadians or United Empire Loyalists, are proud of their traditions and their history.

A fishing village on the coast of New Brunswick

A campsite in Cape Breton Highlands National Park, NS

Louisbourg on Cape Breton Island, NS

Some Maritimers of Scottish descent still speak Gaelic. Traditional Highland Games are held, bagpipes are played and the children learn Scottish songs and dances. There is a small black population, descended from slaves who escaped from the United States before and during the Civil War.

In Nova Scotia and New Brunswick there is rich farmland near the coast and in the river valleys, and the highlands are richly forested. Nova Scotia is almost surrounded by the sea. A causeway joins the mainland peninsula to Cape Breton Island where John Cabot may have landed in 1497. An outstandingly beautiful highway along the north coast is named the Cabot Trail. Halifax, the capital of Nova Scotia, is Canada's chief naval base and has large shipbuilding yards.

There are many historic sites in the province. Louisbourg, once the most heavily fortified French fortress in the New World, is being restored, and a replica of the *Habitation*, the first French settlement in Acadia, has been built on the original site.

A Prince Edward Island farmer storing hay in his barn

An Island farm

Green Gables House

The narrow bay of Fundy which separates the Nova Scotia peninsula from New Brunswick has dramatic ocean tides which sometimes rise more than 50 feet (15 m) at the head of the bay. The great tides rush into the rivers in a high wall of water called a "bore". At the mouth of the Saint John River, at the famous Reversing Falls, the high tide is so strong that it pushes the water backward over the falls.

Prince Edward Island is often called simply "the Island". Although it is the smallest, both in population and area, it is the most densely populated of all the provinces of Canada. The low, rolling landscape is covered in rich red soil and most of the land is cultivated. Tidy fields stretch to the sea. Many of the houses have high roofs and gables and are painted white. This is the country of *Anne of Green Gables*. Lucy Maud Montgomery who wrote the *Anne* books lived on the Island and her home is preserved there.

24

Quebec still has many fine old stone houses like this one

Bic, an old French-Canadian village

Quebec

Quebec is the largest province of Canada and has a population of more than six million people. Most of them are French Canadians descended from the settlers of New France. About 11 per cent are of British descent, and others have come from European countries and the United States. French is spoken by almost everyone and about one quarter of the people speak both English and French.

The motto of Quebec is "Je me souviens", "I remember". The people remember the courage and endurance of their ancestors and they are proud of their traditions and their French-Canadian culture. The early French colonists struggled to survive in a harsh climate, often under attack by hostile Indians. Nevertheless their farms, towns and cities grew. Religious orders established schools and hospitals, and missionaries worked among the Indian tribes.

The handsome decorations and furniture of an old house in Quebec City

There were no new immigrants from France after 1759, and French-Canadian life developed separately from life in France. The Roman Catholic Church continued to have a great influence. The parish priest was a man of tremendous importance and the church was the focus of community life. The Church's influence is still strong, especially in rural areas and religion plays an important part in family life. Children are brought up rather more strictly than in other parts of Canada, and family ties are strong.

Some of the old stone cottages of Quebec are still inhabited, and covered bridges and outdoor ovens are seen in country areas. The ancient crafts of woodcarving, embroidery and weaving are very much alive, and the smell of home-made bread issues from country kitchens. Yet Montreal is a sophisticated modern city and the Lower St Lawrence Valley is a busy industrial region.

Since Confederation the people of Quebec have played an active part in Canadian life. However, there has always been rivalry between English-speaking and French-speaking Canadians. Today about sixteen million Canadians are English-speaking and about six million, most of them living in the province of Quebec, are French-speaking. English and French have equal status as official languages in Canada but Quebec is the only province where the majority speak French.

In the early 1960s some French Canadians began to urge vigorously that Quebec should separate from the rest of Canada to become an independent French-speaking country. Since that time Separatism has been an important movement in the province. All French Canadians agree that French must be unchallenged as the predominant language of Quebec. However, most of them wish Quebec to remain a French-speaking province of Canada.

The early colonists settled on the flat fertile land near the St Lawrence River which remains a great trade route and a

A covered bridge

Collecting maple syrup

An ice sculpture made for Quebec's winter carnival

gateway to the sea. Many farms still stretch in long narrow strips from the river, with the farmhouses standing close together on the road.

The Lower St Lawrence Valley is still the heartland of the province. The best farming land is there and the region is the most industrialized and densely populated in Quebec. To the north lie the highlands of the Canadian Shield.

Most of Canada's maple syrup comes from Quebec, from the area south of the St Lawrence River. In the spring the sap of the maple trees is harvested and people gather for the Festival of the Spring Syrup. The sap is boiled for hours until it turns to syrup. Everyone joins in the party and tastes the hot fresh syrup.

The 24 June, the festival of St Jean Baptiste (John the Baptist), the patron saint of the province, is a public holiday in Quebec. There are gay festivities and processions through the streets. In Montreal the celebrations continue for a week.

Steps join the Upper and Lower Towns of Quebec City

Quebec City

Quebec City is the provincial capital, built on a great rock overlooking the St Lawrence River. The Lower Town lies on the waterfront, on a narrow strip of land below the rock. The streets are narrow and many of the houses are hundreds of years old. The Upper Town is on high ground and the oldest part of it is partly surrounded by a stone wall. Quebec is the only walled city in Canada. Tourists come to see the historic buildings and to eat in the fine restaurants.

The Citadel, completed by the British in 1832, is a mighty fortress overlooking the city. Today it is the summer residence of the Governor General of Canada. Nearby a spacious park covers the Plains of Abraham, the famous battlefield where New France was won by the British in 1759.

Icebreakers keep the port of Quebec open all year and there are many industries. Modern suburbs stretch beyond the Upper Town. Nearly all the citizens are French Canadians and their winter carnival is famous throughout North America.

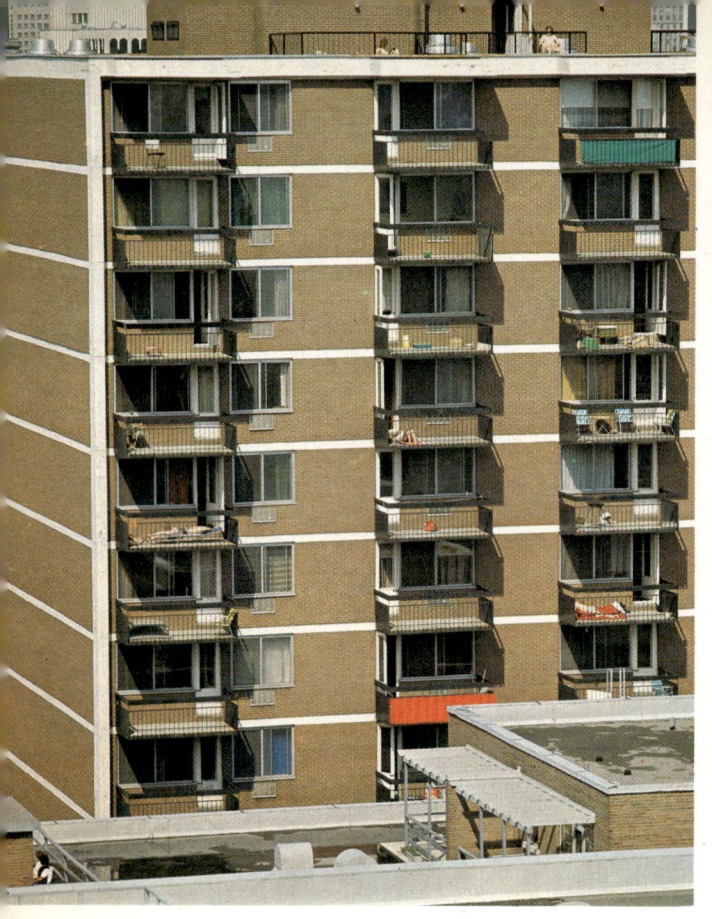

LEFT and RIGHT: New and old apartments in Montreal

Montreal, built on an island in the St Lawrence River, is the largest city in Canada and the second largest French-speaking city in the world. Many buildings in the old part of the city near the waterfront date from the days of New France. At the same time high-rise buildings, bustling streets and luxurious hotels show that Montreal is a flourishing modern city. Half Quebec's industry lies in the Montreal area, and the city is one of the largest inland ports in the world.

Mount Royal, from which the city gets its name, rises in the middle of the island. People enjoy skiing and other winter sports on Mount Royal, and in summer horse-drawn carriages take visitors there for a fine view of the city. In 1967 Expo 67, a lavish international exhibition, was held in Montreal, and the city was chosen as the site of the 1976 Summer Olympics.

Ontario

One-third of Canada's population lives in Ontario, mostly in the industrial cities and towns and the rich farming communities near the Upper St Lawrence River and the Great Lakes. This is the most southerly part of Canada. The Niagara peninsula has tobacco fields, orchards, vineyards and a flourishing wine industry.

Southern Ontario was first explored by the French. The first settlers were the United Empire Loyalists and immigrants from Britian and Europe who came in the early nineteenth century. Museums show how the pioneers lived and worked. At Upper Canada Village, near Morrisburg, authentic old homes, workshops and farm buildings have been collected to create a typical rural community of the early nineteenth century. Southern Ontario has grown from a colony of pioneer farmers to become one of the busiest industrial areas of the world. Half of Canada's manufactured goods are produced there.

Sweet corn on sale from an Ontario farm

Niagara Falls. The American Falls are to the left and the Canadian Horseshoe Falls to the right

The Great Lakes, with their inland ports and manufacturing cities such as Kingston, Toronto and Hamilton, are important to Canada's prosperity. They provide a trade route to the United States and, since the St Lawrence Seaway was opened, to Europe and the rest of the world. Niagara Falls, on the Niagara River between Lakes Erie and Ontario, is one of the most spectacular waterfalls in the world. Millions of tourists visit the Falls each year, many of them honeymoon couples from both Canada and the United States. The Welland Canal bypasses the Falls and allows ships to sail between Lake Erie and Lake Ontario. The tremendous power of the waterfall is used to generate electricity.

To the north Ontario extends across the Canadian Shield to James Bay and Hudson Bay, and to the west it stretches along the north shores of Lakes Huron and Superior, almost to the edge of the Prairie. The richest mining region is around Sudbury, and Ontario has the world's largest uranium mine at Elliot Lake.

Today about 60 per cent of the people in Ontario are of British descent and 10 per cent are French. Others have come from all over the world to enrich the life of the province with their energy and traditions. More than half the immigrants who have come to Canada since 1945 have settled in Ontario, many of them in the city of Toronto.

Every European language may be heard in Toronto. New Canadians tend to live in districts where people speak their own language. The children learn English at school, but at home they speak such languages as Greek, Hungarian or Italian with their parents.

Many New Canadians continue their traditional crafts, customs and religious celebrations. Across the country folk festivals are held, and often, at country fairs, trade and agricultural exhibitions, and on special occasions, songs and dances are performed from Scotland, Ireland, the Ukraine, Germany and many other countries.

New Canadians from Bulgaria dancing in national costume

Toronto Stock Exchange

A factory making outboard motors

The Toronto skyline reflected by the walls of the new City Hall

Toronto, on the north shore of Lake Ontario, is the capital city of Ontario and the second largest city in Canada. Lying in the middle of Ontario's manufacturing region, it is the leading business community in Canada as well as a busy port and air terminal.

The city slopes upward from the waterfront. The heart of the city is a vigorous mixture of modern skyscrapers, fine public buildings, hotels, elegant stores and, on Yonge Street, gaudy neon signs and souvenir shops. The new City Hall, opened in 1964, is an outstanding landmark. Nathan Phillips Square in front of City Hall has a public skating rink in winter, and thousands gather there on New Year's Eve.

On summer week-ends people can escape from the heat of the city to Toronto Island and the other small islands off the shore, where they can relax on the beaches or take a sailing-boat on to Lake Ontario.

The Prairie Provinces

Manitoba, Saskatchewan and Alberta are known as the "Prairie Provinces" because of the great fertile plain which covers one-third of the area. Winters here are long and severe, summers short and hot. The extremes of temperature recorded in Winnipeg are 108 °F (42 °C) and −54 °F (−48 °C). Strong, biting winds often bring added discomfort in winter. However, pure dry air, brilliant sunshine and clear blue skies compensate for the harsh temperatures and make the Prairie an invigorating place to live.

Millions of buffalo once grazed on the grasslands of the Prairie. Today the region is world famous for farming, and especially for its wheat crop. The landscape has a special beauty. The smooth flat farmland stretches to the horizon in every direction. Above is a wide expanse of sky. Farmhouses are widely scattered, and the skyline is broken only by the low buildings and tall grain elevators of the small towns which have grown up beside the railway.

Grain elevators in a small Alberta town. Grain is stored in the elevators until it can be taken by rail to the ports or flour-mills

Beef-cattle ranch

Dairy cows on a Manitoba farm

The history of the Prairie Provinces began with the Plains Indians, the fur traders, the Métis and the pioneers of the Red River Colony who made the hazardous journey from Hudson Bay to present-day Winnipeg in 1812.

After the completion of the Canadian Pacific Railway in 1885, pioneers came from every country in Europe, many of them from the Ukraine, Germany and Poland. Icelanders founded fishing villages on the shores of Lake Winnipeg, Jews came from Eastern Europe, and Protestants, such as the Mennonites and Hutterites, fled persecution in Russia and set up colonies where they farmed and lived a simple communal life.

Today less than half the people of the Prairie Provinces are of British descent, and new Canadians are still coming from many different countries. There are a number of French-speaking communities, especially in Manitoba. French Canadians in St Boniface, now part of the city of Winnipeg,

Giant combines harvesting wheat

hold their own winter carnival, the *Festival du Voyageur*, celebrating the days of the fur traders and the early French settlers.

Winnipeg, capital of Manitoba, is the oldest and largest city on the Prairie and is still called "the Gateway to the West". It is the marketing city for western grain and, like all Prairie cities, it has such food industries as flour-mills, meat-packing plants and canning factories. In winter the intersection of Portage Avenue and Main Street is said to be the coldest and windiest street corner in Canada, but in summer 90 °F (32 °C) temperatures often chase Winnipeggers out of the city to the shores of Lake Winnipeg nearby.

Alberta has rich deposits of oil and natural gas, and the oil industry has encouraged rapid growth in the cities of Edmonton and Calgary. Some of the smaller Prairie towns have fascinating names such as Moose Jaw, Medicine Hat and Indian Head.

These Hutterite children still dress in the same style as their ancestors

The Centennial Concert Hall in Winnipeg

An oil well in the middle of an Alberta farm

Fur trading and colonial days are recalled at Lower Fort Garry, a fortified trading post built by the Hudson's Bay Company on the Red River near Winnipeg, and restored as it was in the mid-nineteenth century. Visitors are fascinated by the store and the fur loft which is stocked with hundreds of skins. Hudson's Bay stores and trading posts still serve many northern settlements, but fur farms now provide two-thirds of the skins for Canada's fur industry.

Rolling farmland stretches beyond the Prairie to the Canadian Shield in the northeast and to the foothills of the mountains in the west. To the southwest rainfall is light and Calgary in Alberta is at the heart of cattle-ranching country. The famous Calgary Stampede is a spectacular annual rodeo and carnival where cowboys compete in bronco riding, bull riding and calf roping, and exciting chuckwagon races are held. Other Prairie towns hold smaller rodeos and fairs during the summer.

Bronco riding at the Calgary Stampede

Rainbow Lake, near Whitehorse, Yukon Territory

The Territories

The Yukon and Northwest Territories occupy one-third of Canada's land area, but they are among the most thinly populated regions of the world.

The Yukon is the most westerly part of Canada. Fur traders reached the Yukon in the mid-nineteenth century. The region became famous when in 1896 gold was discovered in the Klondike. Men came from all over the world to seek their fortune there. They faced tremendous hardships to reach the gold-fields, for there were no roads or railways. Many struggled on foot through icy mountain passes from Alaska to reach Dawson City, the bustling town which sprang up in the heart of the gold-fields. After about three years the boom was over, most of the miners went home, and Dawson City became a quiet town.

Today, Discovery Day, 17 August, is a holiday in the Yukon. In Dawson City everyone wears turn-of-the-century costume and tourists join the local people to celebrate the days of the Gold Rush.

An isolated settlement

Eskimo children on their way to school

Travel and tourism in the Yukon have become easier since the construction of the Alaska Highway. This great highway, 1520 miles (2446 km) long, was built during the Second World War to provide a safe inland route from the north of British Columbia, across the Yukon, to the American territory of Alaska.

Most of Canada's northern coastline and all the Arctic islands lie within the Northwest Territories. The winters are so cold and long, and summer temperatures so cool that trees cannot grow in most of the region. There are vast areas of tundra, a treeless plain where the ground below the surface is permanently frozen.

Food and supplies are delivered by air or by boat from the south. In summer the Arctic Ocean and the Mackenzie River are the main water routes, and there are now small modern towns on the coast and in the Mackenzie Valley. About half of the people in the Northwest Territories are Indian or Eskimo, many of them living in isolated communities which depend on shortwave radio to communicate with the outside world.

British Columbia

British Columbia is cut off from the rest of Canada by high mountain ranges. The temperate Pacific coastal region was first explored by Russian, Spanish and British sailors, and it was not until 1793 that the first European, Alexander Mackenzie, reached the Pacific coast overland.

A British colony was established on Vancouver Island in 1849, and on the mainland in 1858 when the Cariboo Gold Rush brought thousands of people to the interior of British Columbia. Most of them came by way of the west coast, but in 1862 a courageous group known as the Overlanders journeyed overland from Ontario. Many of them did not find gold, but they stayed as farmers, fishermen or lumbermen. The promise that the Canadian Pacific Railway would be built, making a permanent link with the rest of Canada, persuaded British Columbia to join the Confederation in 1871.

The Trans-Canada Highway snaking its way through the passes of the Rocky Mountains

Making paper from British Columbia's trees is a major industry. This paper mill is on Vancouver Island

British Columbia is a young, vigorous province, enormously rich in forests, minerals and water power. The Fraser Valley is a fertile farming area and the Okanagan Valley is famous for fruit growing. The mountain scenery is magnificent, and the Pacific coast is especially beautiful. Thickly forested mountains rise from the sea. The coast is cut by narrow inlets and there are many offshore islands. Tourism is an important industry throughout the province.

Victoria, the capital, is on the southern tip of Vancouver Island, and is linked to the mainland by air and ferry services. It is a port and a fishing and lumbering town. The flower gardens are outstanding and in summer flower baskets hang from the lamp posts. Many people, especially from British Columbia and the Prairie Provinces, move to Victoria when they retire to enjoy the mild climate.

Double-decker buses and flower baskets in British Columbia's capital, Victoria

Vancouver from English Bay

Vancouver, the largest city and busiest port in British Columbia, is beautifully situated on the mainland, close to the mountains and the sea. The great forests stretch right to the outskirts of the city. Most of the people earn their living in industries connected with the forests or the sea, in sawmills, pulp and paper mills, fish-processing plants or shipbuilding yards.

Stanley Park, the city's largest park, is famous for its natural beauty, its zoo and the Indian totem poles which stand there. Vancouver's fine sandy beaches are crowded in summer. Plants flourish here which cannot survive the cold winters elsewhere in Canada, and almost everyone grows flowers.

Most British Columbians are of British descent but there are large numbers of people from other European countries. Vancouver has a large Chinese community and there are many Canadians of Japanese origin living in the province.

ABOVE A Christmas display in a Montreal Park. BELOW Clearing snow. RIGHT A hooded parka keeps children warm

Daily Life in the Seasons

Every aspect of life in Canada is influenced by the climate. In winter snow may be on the ground for six months on the Prairie, and for up to four months in eastern Canada. Rivers and lakes are frozen and the streets and highways are kept open by huge snow-clearing machines.

On calm sunny days families dress up warmly and set off with toboggans and skates for an afternoon of fun in the fresh air. When the weather is cold and dry, the snow is powdery, and children can roll and play in it without getting wet. A popular outing is a Tallyho, a ride in a horse-drawn sleigh.

Winter clothing has to be light and warm. Every child wears a hooded parka with a thick pile or quilted lining. This is a modern version of the Eskimo parka, designed to keep out freezing winds and blowing snow in conditions when the tip of an ear can freeze quickly if it is not protected.

Policemen in Winnipeg used to wear ankle-length coats of buffalo hide when they were outside in winter.

Winter is hard for elderly people and mothers with young children, because it is often too cold and icy for them to go out. Perhaps this is why Canadians use the telephone so much. People who have to stay at home do not feel so isolated if they can talk with their friends on the telephone.

Of course, blizzards, ice or deep snow sometimes disrupt everyday life. On the whole, however, Canadians carry on as usual in winter. In the suburban shopping areas, people can park their cars and then walk from store to store in a covered, heated mall. On the Prairie, where the temperature may be intensely cold for several weeks at a time, people plug their cars into the electricity supply when they are not being driven. The electric current warms the engine, charges the battery and keeps the inside of the car warm.

Bonhomme Carnaval is the symbol of Quebec's winter carnival

Ships frozen in on the St Lawrence Seaway

Boys clearing snow from the porch roof

Winnipeg houses decorated for Christmas

Spring mud

Christmas and New Year festivities bring warmth and light to the middle of the Canadian winter. For everyone Christmas is a time when families get together, great feasts are prepared and gifts exchanged. Young children believe that Santa Claus comes from the North Pole on Christmas Eve in his reindeer-drawn sleigh to deliver the gifts.

City streets, public buildings and private homes are brightly decorated. Lighted Christmas trees stand on snow-covered lawns and in unshaded windows. Many families go into the provincial forests to cut down their own Christmas trees, and Canada exports Christmas trees to many countries.

Spring is a short season in Canada. When the snow turns to slush and mud, mothers buy rubber boots for their children and hope that the ground will dry out quickly. Lawns slowly turn green again. Suddenly the trees burst into leaf and Canadians realize with delight that summer has come again.

Summer too is short, but it is a glorious season in Canada. Schools close during July and August, and everyone enjoys a few weeks of relaxed and casual living. Canadians seize every opportunity to be outdoors. The stores are filled with barbecues, camping equipment and garden furniture for the long hot sunny days and warm nights.

Every large city is within a few hours' drive of unspoiled natural countryside. At week-ends and holidays families leave for the lakes, the mountains or the sea. Camping is very popular, and there are many well-equipped camping and picnic grounds, planned to blend into the natural surroundings. Deer often wander into the camps and resort areas, and the occasional black bear comes to look for scraps of food.

Many families have their own summer cabin in the wilderness, or a cottage at a summer townsite on the lake shore. Churches and youth groups run excellent summer camps for children and young people where the youngsters live in simple cabins or tents.

A summer home in Alberta

Boys in their tree house

Raking up the fallen leaves

Fall (autumn) is often the most beautiful season of the year. The countryside is ablaze with crimson and gold, and flowers in city gardens bloom until the first severe frost. The warm mellow days of "Indian Summer" often last into October. Children play in the fallen leaves until it is time to rake them up before the snow comes.

Crops grow and ripen quickly in the long summer days, and in September and early October farmers hurry to gather the harvest before the onset of winter. Thanksgiving Day, the second Monday of October, is a public holiday. The pioneers of North America brought with them the European custom of the Harvest Festival, and they made it a time of thanksgiving for all the blessings the year had brought in a new land. Thanksgiving Day is still celebrated in this tradition. Church services are held, and families gather for a meal of turkey, cranberry sauce and pumpkin pie.

Hallowe'en, on 31 October, long known in Europe as the time when witches ride, has become an evening of fun for young children. After dark they dress up in costume and go from door to door, threatening to play tricks unless they are given "treats" of apples or candy.

48

Sport

Ice hockey is the most popular sport in Canada, and Canadian hockey teams are among the best in the world. The climate in Canada is splendid for training. Boys can play on outside ice in winter and every district has its boys' hockey league. In the indoor arenas ice can be maintained throughout the year. Professional hockey teams have enthusiastic support and many games are shown on television.

Canadians excel in competitive skating and skiing. Curling, a team sport on ice, is played by both men and women. A curling competition is called a *bonspiel*, and in the National Bonspiel the provinces compete for the MacDonald Brier Trophy.

Lacrosse, a fast field sport developed from a game played by Canadian Indians, is played in Canada but is not widely popular. Snowshoeing, the old Indian way of crossing deep snow, is still a valuable skill in the wilderness, and some Canadians enjoy snowshoeing for fun in winter. Cross-country skiing and, more recently, snowmobiling also provide plenty of outdoor excitement.

In spring and summer baseball, tennis, golf and water sports are

Ice hockey

A boy dressed for a hockey game

popular. Nearly everyone lives near a lake, a river or the sea, so it is important for children to learn to swim and to follow rules for safety in the water.

    Canadian football is played with an oval-shaped ball and is much like American football, although the rules are slightly different. Each major city has a professional team. The football season, which runs from August to November, ends with the most spectacular sports event in Canada, the Grey Cup Game, when the winning teams from Eastern and Western Canada compete for the national championship. Rivalry between East and West is intense, and spectators come from all over the country. The Grey Cup Game is played on a Sunday so that the greatest number of people can watch on television. When the victorious players return to their home town, they receive a heroes' welcome.

Boys playing Canadian football

Homes

Canadians like to live in a house while their children are growing up, though apartments or flats are popular with young married couples, single people and the elderly. Residential districts have schools, churches, stores and playgrounds all within easy reach.

Except in the temperate climate of British Columbia, homes have to be built to withstand very cold temperatures. Central heating, insulation and double windows are essential. In summer mesh screens over the windows keep out mosquitoes and flies. Foundations must be sunk below the level to which frost penetrates in winter so that the building remains stable as the earth freezes and thaws. As a result, every home has a basement which provides storage room and an indoor play area in winter. Often a family room or workshop is built in the basement, and space is used for laundry equipment and winter clothes drying.

A home in the mountains of British Columbia

Putting up the storm windows

Apartment balconies

Modern Canadian homes are designed for informal living. Housework is made easier by numerous electrical appliances, particularly in the kitchen. Homes are automatically kept at an even temperature of about 70 °F (21 °C) by central heating systems burning oil or natural gas.

City-dwellers buy most of their food from large supermarkets which have parking space for cars. Many stores remain open until 9 p.m. and it is not unusual to see husbands shopping in the evening. Usually groceries are bought weekly, since refrigerators and freezers allow food to be stored easily at home.

A thick juicy steak with a baked potato and salad is considered a fine meal in Canada, though children usually prefer the characteristic North American hamburger or hot dog. French-Canadian cooking is superb and Canadians of different origins all have their own special recipes. Specialty shops sell such exotic foods as vine leaves or bamboo shoots, as well as cooked meats, sausages and pastries of all kinds.

Building a timber-framed house

A gourmet cheese shop in Ontario

A language class for adults

Education

Canada has two official languages, English and French. Speeches in Parliament may be given in either language. Government documents and product labels are printed in both languages and there are English and French services in radio and television. In school most Canadian children are taught in English, but French-speaking children in Quebec and some other provinces are taught in French. Of course their books are written in French too, and they study French and French-Canadian rather than English literature and history. As far as possible children learn the other official language in school, so that more and more Canadians are able to speak both English and French. Canadians speak with a distinctive Canadian accent, and typically Canadian words and expressions occur in both languages.

One-third of all Canadians are of neither British nor French descent. Immigrants are encouraged to attend free language classes in English or French, but many foreign-born Canadians are still more comfortable speaking their native language. In western Canada especially there are weekly newspapers published in languages such as German, Ukrainian, Icelandic and Yiddish.

Students outside a high school in Quebec

All over Canada public notices are in both French and English

  Each province in Canada has its own school system. Quebec and Newfoundland provide separate schools for Roman Catholics and Protestants, but elsewhere each community has a public school which is open to everyone. Education is free and compulsory from the ages of six to sixteen in most provinces.

  Most Canadian children have an elementary school for the six to twelve-year-olds near their home, but in rural areas older students may have to travel many miles by bus to the nearest high school. In the far north and other thinly populated districts, students may have to live away from home during the week or even for the entire term, because their school is so far away.

  Nearly all schools teach boys and girls together. Every class elects its own president and secretary, and in high school the students plan their own social activities. High schools, which may take up to two thousand students, offer a wide variety of subjects, and students have to work hard if they wish to graduate with distinction in their final year.

When they leave high school, about one-third of Canadian youngsters go on to further full-time education at a university or vocational college. Many universities today are on the outskirts of a large city, with a variety of modern buildings, lecture halls, student residences, libraries and laboratories, set in spacious grounds. Laval University in Quebec City, founded in 1663, is the oldest university in Canada, while Toronto is the largest with over twenty-two thousand full-time undergraduate students.

Students of universities and vocational colleges must pay fees which cover part of the cost of their education. Scholarships, bursaries and loans are available, but students often work in the long summer vacation to earn their fees and living expenses for the coming year. There is always seasonal work in Canada during the summer, and students are employed in hotels, resort areas, national parks and lumber camps, as well as in industry.

Students at Simon Fraser University, British Columbia

A string of barges on the Mackenzie River

The port of Montreal, the entrance to the St Lawrence Seaway

An ore-carrying train on the Great Slave Lake Railway, NWT

Transport

The rivers and lakes were Canada's first transport routes. The Indians, fur traders, explorers and early settlers used them, carrying their boats and supplies past dangerous rapids and waterfalls, and sometimes for considerable distances from one waterway to the next. These carrying places were called *portages*. In summer the rivers and lakes are still the north's main surface routes.

Today the most important water route is the St Lawrence Seaway, linking the Great Lakes to the Atlantic Ocean. The Seaway, completed in 1959, was a joint project by Canada and the United States. It provides a channel deep enough to allow ocean-going ships to sail inland up the St Lawrence River to all the Great Lakes. Kingston, Toronto and Hamilton are now ocean ports. From Thunder Bay on Lake Superior, 2300 miles (3710 km) from the sea, grain can be shipped direct to Europe. Unfortunately the Seaway is frozen in winter.

A wide-ranging network of roads and railways now serves the populated parts of Canada. In 1962 the Trans-Canada Highway was completed to cover 4860 miles (7820 km) from St John's, Newfoundland, to Victoria, British Columbia. In the north winter roads are constructed each year when the ground is frozen hard. The roads turn to mud in the spring and are rebuilt each year.

People in a hurry travel by air in Canada. It takes three days to go from Montreal to Vancouver by train, but only about five hours by plane. Small airlines take freight and passengers to isolated settlements in the north. Occasionally a small plane is lost in the wilderness and a highly efficient air search and rescue service goes into action. Pilots who fly in the north need special training, and they must carry emergency supplies in case of accident.

The Trans-Canada Highway crossing the Prairies

The Mackenzie Highway after the spring thaw

Winter transport in the north—snowmobiles beside a plane which has landed on the frozen sea

The huge aluminium (aluminum) smelting plant at Kitimat in the north of British Columbia

Industry

Canada has immense natural resources. Mining, fishing, forestry and farming are great sources of wealth and provide raw materials for manufacturing industries. Pulp and paper production is the leading industry. More newsprint (paper for newspapers) is produced in Canada than in any other country in the world. Other important industries are the manufacture of cars and trucks, farm machinery, iron and steel, machine tools, electrical equipment and food products.

Rich deposits of copper, gold, iron, lead, platinum, asbestos, potash, silver, zinc, uranium and nickel are all found in Canada. Western Canada has large reserves of coal, oil and natural gas, and water power generates most of the country's electricity.

Fishing is one of Canada's oldest industries. Atlantic and Pacific coastal waters yield salmon, cod, haddock, herring, halibut and sole, as well as fine lobster, oysters and other shellfish. The inland lakes provide freshwater fish, with Arctic char and smoked Lake Winnipeg goldeye as particular delicacies.

Enormous forests make lumbering one of Canada's most productive industries. There have been logging camps in the Canadian forest since colonial days, and the work is hard and lonely. The lumberjacks who cut down the trees are highly respected for their strength and courage. Each tree is felled separately, and a skilled man can make a huge tree fall exactly where he wants it, clear of other trees and stumps which might damage it. In British Columbia, which produces more than two-thirds of Canada's lumber, the Douglas fir can grow to a height of more than 200 feet (60 m), with a trunk 4 or 5 feet (nearly 1.5 m) across.

Timber ready to be transported to the mills

The remote Arctic coastline of Canada's wilderness

The Canadian Wilderness

Much of Canada's most magnificent countryside has been preserved for all time in its natural state in the national and provincial parks. The first national park was created near the mineral hot springs in Banff, Alberta, in the Rocky Mountains. There are now extensive areas of national parkland in the mountains of Alberta and British Columbia.

The towering peaks and valleys, the glaciers, beautiful lakes, rivers and waterfalls remain unspoiled. Wild animals and plant life are protected. Deer, elk, moose, beaver, black and grizzly bears, smaller animals like chipmunks, marmots and skunks, as well as a tremendous variety of birds, live undisturbed in their natural surroundings. Park naturalists, employed by the Canadian Government, explain the natural history and the wildlife of the region to visitors. National and provincial parks have been established across the country in some of the most beautiful areas of every province.

Outside the national and provincial parks there are seasons for hunting and shooting. Many a father returns from a hunting trip in the fall with his quota of venison and moose meat to stock the family's freezer. Fishing can be fun for the whole family, especially the delicious treat of fresh fish cooked and eaten in the open air.

Campers and sportsmen who venture far from civilization must know how to survive in the wilderness and be prepared for sudden changes in the weather.

A few adventurous people travel by canoe, welcoming the quiet, the solitude and the challenge of the northland.

For the future the wilderness offers abundant treasure. Immense wealth in minerals and water power awaits development. At the same time the peace and natural beauty of the land promises continuing refreshment of the spirit for Canadians and their visitors.

Scientists exploring Baffin Island measure the ice's thickness

Sportsmen catching a salmon

Some facts and figures

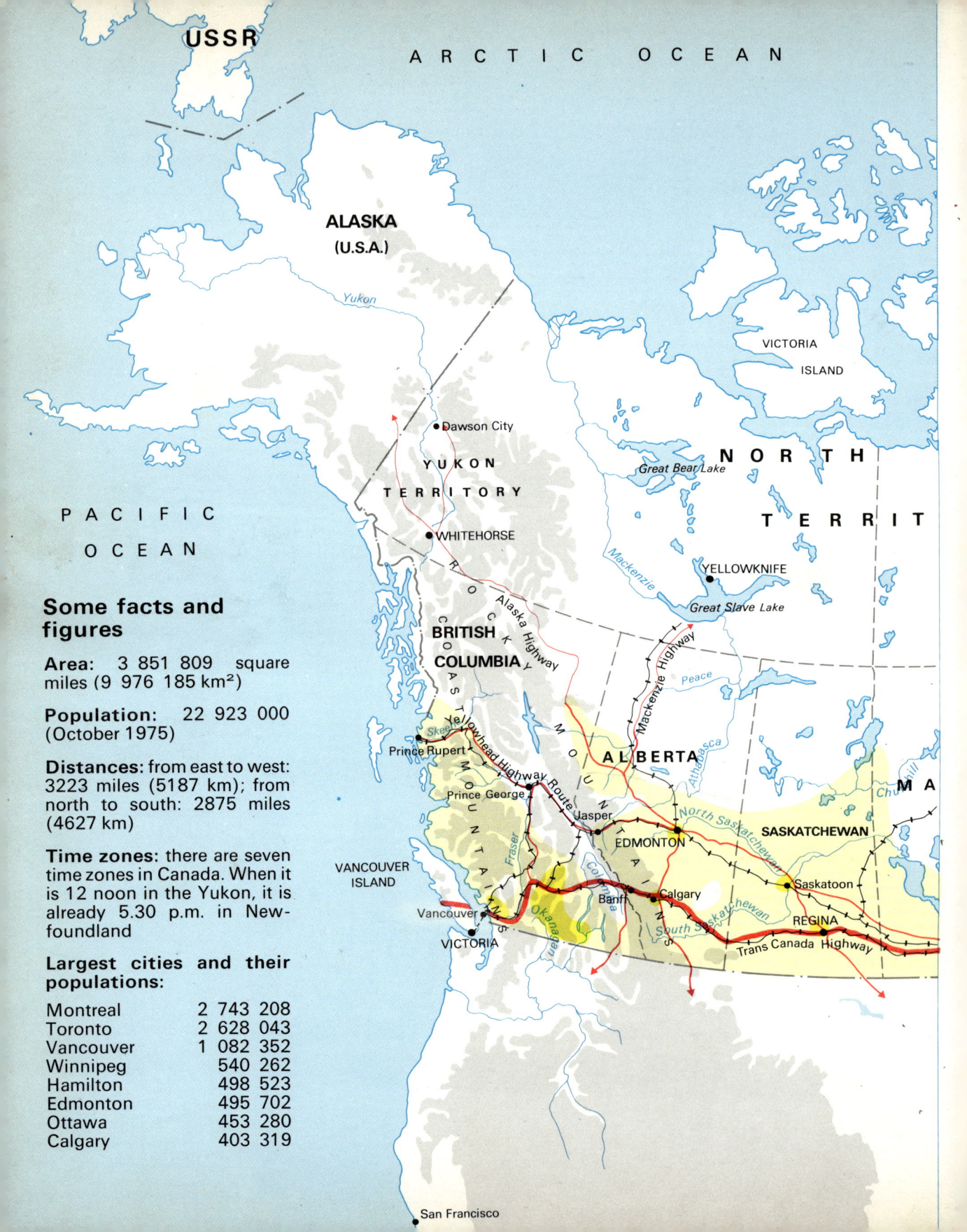

Area: 3 851 809 square miles (9 976 185 km²)

Population: 22 923 000 (October 1975)

Distances: from east to west: 3223 miles (5187 km); from north to south: 2875 miles (4627 km)

Time zones: there are seven time zones in Canada. When it is 12 noon in the Yukon, it is already 5.30 p.m. in Newfoundland

Largest cities and their populations:

Montreal	2 743 208
Toronto	2 628 043
Vancouver	1 082 352
Winnipeg	540 262
Hamilton	498 523
Edmonton	495 702
Ottawa	453 280
Calgary	403 319

the Canadian Government, explain the natural history and the wildlife of the region to visitors. National and provincial parks have been established across the country in some of the most beautiful areas of every province.

Outside the national and provincial parks there are seasons for hunting and shooting. Many a father returns from a hunting trip in the fall with his quota of venison and moose meat to stock the family's freezer. Fishing can be fun for the whole family, especially the delicious treat of fresh fish cooked and eaten in the open air.

Campers and sportsmen who venture far from civilization must know how to survive in the wilderness and be prepared for sudden changes in the weather.

A few adventurous people travel by canoe, welcoming the quiet, the solitude and the challenge of the northland.

For the future the wilderness offers abundant treasure. Immense wealth in minerals and water power awaits development. At the same time the peace and natural beauty of the land promises continuing refreshment of the spirit for Canadians and their visitors.

Scientists exploring Baffin Island measure the ice's thickness

Sportsmen catching a salmon

Some facts and figures

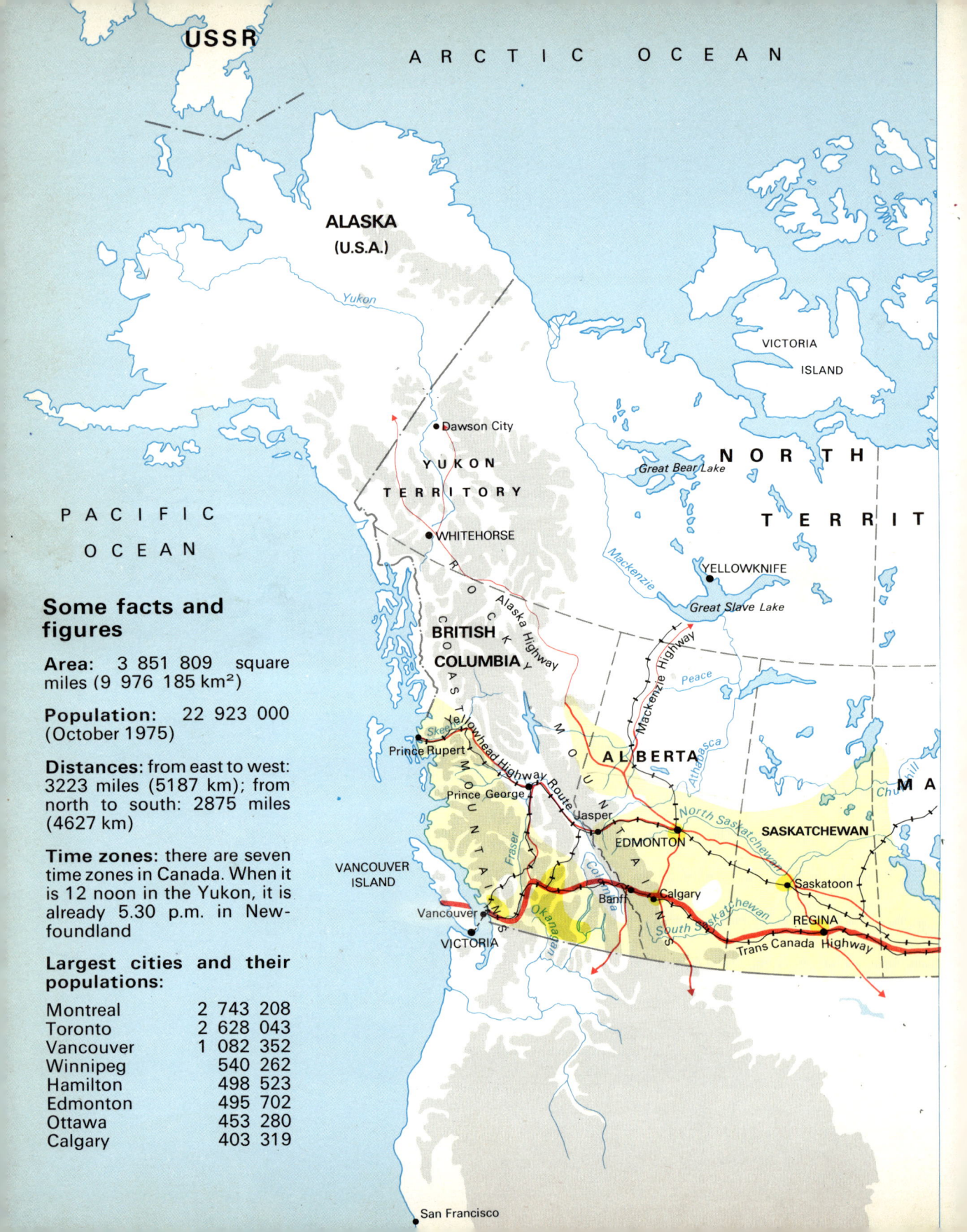

Area: 3 851 809 square miles (9 976 185 km²)

Population: 22 923 000 (October 1975)

Distances: from east to west: 3223 miles (5187 km); from north to south: 2875 miles (4627 km)

Time zones: there are seven time zones in Canada. When it is 12 noon in the Yukon, it is already 5.30 p.m. in Newfoundland

Largest cities and their populations:

Montreal	2 743 208
Toronto	2 628 043
Vancouver	1 082 352
Winnipeg	540 262
Hamilton	498 523
Edmonton	495 702
Ottawa	453 280
Calgary	403 319

Main railways
Main roads
International boundaries
Provincial boundaries
Land over 1000 metres
Number of people to 1 square mile (2.6 km²)
less than 1
1–30
more than 30
Federal capital
N
GREENLAND
(DENMARK)
ELLESMERE ISLAND
BAFFIN ISLAND
WEST
ORIES
ATLANTIC
OCEAN
Hudson Strait
Hudson Bay
NEWFOUNDLAND
Churchill
Churchill
QUEBEC
NITOBA
Nelson
James Bay
Lake Winnipeg
ONTARIO
Gulf of St. Lawrence
GRAND BANKS
ST. JOHN'S
PRINCE EDWARD ISLAND
CAPE BRETON ISLAND
St. Lawrence
NEW BRUNSWICK
CHARLOTTETOWN
QUEBEC
FREDERICTON
Saint John
NOVA SCOTIA
HALIFAX
WINNIPEG
Thunder Bay
Lake Superior
Ottawa
Montreal
Bay of Fundy
Sudbury
OTTAWA
Red
Lake Huron
Kingston
Boston
TORONTO
L. Ontario
Hamilton
Niagara Falls
Lake Michigan
Detroit
Windsor
L. Erie
New York
Chicago
miles
0 100 200 300 400 500
0 100 200 300 400 500 600 700 800
kilometres

Index

Acadia 12, 13, 22, 23
Alaska Highway 40
Alberta 14, 35–38
Arctic 6, 10, 11, 13, 40, 60, 61
Arctic Winter Games 10
Atlantic Ocean 6, 22, 56

Baffin Island 61
Banff 60
Black Creek Pioneer Village 15
British Columbia 13, 14, 41–43, 51, 55, 59, 60
buffalo 8, 9, 35, 45

Cabot, John 12, 23
Calgary 37, 38
camping 9, 47, 61
Canadian Pacific Railway 15, 36
Canadian Shield 7, 28, 32, 38
Cariboo Gold Rush 41
Cartier, Jacques 12
Cape Breton Island 12, 23
Champlain, Samuel de 12
Charlottetown 14
Citadel 29
Columbus, Christopher 8
curling 49

Dawson City 39
Douglas fir 59

Edmonton 16, 37
Elizabeth, Queen 17
Elliot Lake 32
Erie, Lake 32
Eskimo 5, 10, 11, 40

farming 21, 23, 24, 28, 31, 35, 38, 42, 58
festivals: Christmas 46; folk 33; New Year 34, 46; religious 33; Thanksgiving 48; Tulip 19
fishing 8, 9, 10, 20, 21, 22, 41, 59, 61
food 52
football 50
Fraser Valley 42
French Canadians 25–29, 53
Fundy, Bay of 24
fur trade 9, 11, 12, 13, 38

Gatineau Hills 17
Government 18–19
Governor General 17, 18, 29
grain elevators 35
Grand Banks 12
Great Lakes 31, 32, 56
Grey Cup 50

Habitation 12, 23
Halifax 23

Hallowe'en 48
Hamilton 32, 56
hockey 49
Hudson Bay 13, 32, 36
Hudson's Bay Company 13, 38
hunting 8, 9, 10, 61
Hutterites 36, 37

icebergs 20
Indians 8–10, 25, 36, 40
industry 21, 28, 30, 31, 37, 43, 58–59
Innuit 10, 11

Kingston 32, 56
Kitimat 58
Klondike 39

Labrador 20
languages 22, 25, 27, 33, 53
Louisbourg 23
Lower Fort Garry 38
lumbering 21, 59

Mackenzie, Alexander 41
Mackenzie River 40, 56
Manitoba 14, 35–38
maple syrup 28
Mennonites 36
Métis 9, 36
mining 21, 32, 58
missionaries 11, 13, 25
Montgomery, Lucy Maud 24
Montreal 12, 26, 28, 30, 44
muskeg 15

National Parks 23, 60, 61
New Brunswick 13, 14, 22–24
New France 12, 13, 25, 29
Newfoundland 12, 14, 20, 21, 54
Niagara Falls 16, 32
Northwest Territories 39, 40
Nova Scotia 13, 14, 22–24

Oil 37, 59
Okanagan Valley 42
Ontario 13, 14, 31–34
Ontario, Lake 32, 34
Ottawa 17–19
outports 20, 21
Overlanders 41

Pacific Coast 7, 8, 13, 15, 41, 42
Pacific Ocean 6
parka 10, 11, 44
Parliament 18, 19
pemmican 8, 9
Plains of Abraham 29
portages 56
Prairie 7, 9, 15, 16, 35–38, 45

Prince Edward Island 6, 13, 14, 22, 24

Quebec 13, 14, 25–29, 53, 54
Quebec City 1, 12, 13, 14, 29
Quebec Separatism 27
Quebec Winter Carnival 29, 45

Red River Colony 13, 36
Reversing Falls 24
Rideau Canal 17
Rideau Hall 17
Riel, Louis 9
Rocky Mountains 7, 41, 60
Royal Canadian Mounted Police 14

St Jean Baptiste 28
Saint John River 24
St John's 20, 57
St Lawrence River 12, 27, 28, 31
St Lawrence Seaway 16, 32, 45, 56
St Lawrence Valley 13, 26, 28
Saskatchewan 14, 35–38
shipbuilding 23, 43
skating 1, 47, 49
skiing 49
snowmobile 11, 49, 57
snowshoes 8, 9, 49
soapstone carvings 5, 11
Stanley Park 43
Sudbury 32
Superior, Lake 56

Tallyho 44
Thunder Bay 56
toboggans 8, 44
Toronto 2, 32, 33, 34, 56
totem poles 8, 43
Trans-Canada Highway 41, 57
tundra 40

United Empire Loyalists 13, 22, 31
United States of America 6, 13, 14, 16, 23, 32, 56
Upper Canada Village 31

Vancouver 43
Vancouver Island 41, 42
Victoria 42, 57
Vikings 12

Welland Canal 32
wheat 7, 35
Winnipeg 36, 37, 45
Winnipeg, Lake 36, 37

Yukon Territory 39, 40

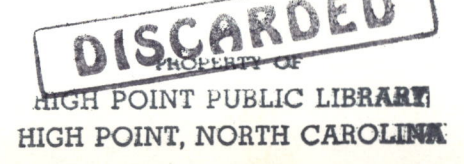

64

212201 J917.1
 E

EARN, JOSEPHINE
 LOOKING AT CANADA.

HIGH POINT PUBLIC
LIBRARY
High Point, North Carolina

DISCARDED